Scrapbooking

OFF THE PAGE . . .
AND ON THE WALL

Martingale®
& COMPANY

Scrapbooking off the Page . . . and on the Wall
© 2006 by Martingale & Company

Martingale & Company
20205 144th Avenue NE
Woodinville, WA 98072-8478 USA
www.martingale-pub.com

Printed in China
11 10 09 08 07 06   8 7 6 5 4 3 2 1

Library of Congress Cataloging-in-Publication Data

Scrapbooking off the page . . . and on the wall.
    p. cm.
   ISBN 1-56477-568-2
  1. Photograph albums. 2. Photographs—Conservation and restoration.
3. Scrapbooks.
   TR465.S3944 2006
   745.593—dc22

2005022745

Credits

President • Nancy J. Martin
CEO • Daniel J. Martin
VP and General Manager • Tom Wierzbicki
Publisher • Jane Hamada
Editorial Director • Mary V. Green
Managing Editor • Tina Cook
Developmental Editor • Dawn Anderson
Technical Editor • Candie Frankel
Copy Editor • Melissa Bryan
Design Director • Stan Green
Illustrator • Laurel Strand
Cover and Text Designer • Shelly Garrison
Photographers • Bill Lindner and Chris McArthur
Photo Stylist • Susan Jorgensen
Photo Assistant • Jason Lund

Credits for Photos Used in Projects

Page 15 (top): Todd and Jennifer King, Expressions Photography, www.expressions-photography.com

Page 25: Keith D. Glasgow, Glasgow Photography, www.glasgowphoto.com

Page 29 (matted photo) and page 39: Stephanie Colgan, Stephanie Colgan Photography, www.colganphotography.com

Page 30: Imad Rhayem, www.madraym.com

Page 33 (framed photo on table) and page 38: Patricia L. Nelson, Just Kids Photography, www.justkidsphotography.com

Page 33 (project photos): Lisa Thies, Favorite Places Photography, www.favoriteplacesphoto.com

Mission Statement
Dedicated to providing quality products and service to inspire creativity.

Contents

Introduction

Scrapbooking is a wonderful way to spotlight the special moments in our lives. Whether it's a new baby, a 50th wedding anniversary, or an evening spent at the pumpkin patch, a scrapbooked page can capture an extraordinary event—or simply a slice of life. In a scrapbook, our memories are placed in a book and put away on a shelf to enjoy from time to time. But what if there was a way to turn those memories into something to enjoy every day?

In *Scrapbooking off the Page . . . and on the Wall*, you'll discover dozens of ideas for transforming your precious photos into amazing, eye-catching displays for your halls, walls, tabletops, and more. These step-by-step projects will inspire you to decorate your own home with tributes to family and friends, and to create personalized heirlooms for everyone on your gift list.

The themes captured within these pages are sure to inspire your first project—or inspire an outing to take photos for your first project! Along with perennial favorite photo subjects such as newborns, siblings, and holidays,

projects spotlight topics such as fishing, baseball, pets, and the beach—everything from an everyday trip to the park to a once-in-a-lifetime vacation.

Traditional scrapbooking presents a page in an album, but you'll find many more creative ways to scrapbook here. Try shadow boxes, photo collages, tile photo transfers, a calendar, an autographed mat, a clip board, and sweet "LOVE" frames that are perfect for gift giving. You can even make a unique memo board out of a shutter!

For many crafters, the most enjoyable part of scrapbooking is choosing and using embellishments. Buttons, twine, seashells, netting, lace, silk flowers, beads, and ribbon are just a few of the trimmings you can play with in these designs. Plus, you'll learn techniques for stamping, sewing, painting, and lettering. Once you master these easy methods, you can springboard "off the page" and create original works of art to display.

So, rescue your photos from those album pages—show them off on your walls instead! You'll be delighted with your handcrafted, photo-filled treasures, and you, your family, and your guests will be able to cherish special times every day of the year.

OUR *Family*

by Gina Hamann

Paint one large and several small canvases. Cut strips of paper in coordinating solid colors. Place the strips side by side, overlapping the edges in an arrangement that will cover the large canvas. Adhere the strips to one another (but not to the canvas). Use a sewing machine to add accent stitching. Mat an enlarged group photo with craft paper. Print a title and verse on solid papers, cut into two ovals, and chalk the edges. Mat each oval, install large eyelets at the sides of one and at the top of the other, and tie with fibers. Cut a piece of solid paper for each small canvas and stitch around the edges. Add a single photo and tie on a charm. Adhere all the pieces to the canvases. Join the small canvases to the large one using screw eyes and hooks.

French Vineyard
SHADOW BOX

by Genevieve A. Sterbenz

Disassemble a shadow box and line the back with suede paper. Mat a vineyard photo on scallop-edged card stock. Mat a wine label on patterned paper. Double-mat a group photo on patterned papers, using raised glue dots between the two mats to add dimension. Arrange and adhere the pieces, including a vineyard-themed postcard, to the background. Accent with champagne glass and wine bottle stickers, die-cut grapes and leaves, a wine cork, and a small stone. Reassemble the shadow box.

Travel
SHADOW BOX

by Saralyn Ewald,
Sr. Designer, Archiver's

Disassemble a shadow box. Line the back with corrugated cardboard and overlay with patterned paper. Cut tags from manila card stock to fill the background when spaced evenly. Punch a hole in each tag, and rub brown chalk ink around the edges. Adhere trip photos, a travel sticker, a section of map, and a dried botany sample to the tags. (For an aged look, photocopy your originals on a sepia-tone setting.) Accent the tags with stamped dates, stickers, a chipboard letter, and a vellum message strip. Adhere the tags to the background, using foam dots to raise them off the surface. Hand print card-stock labels and mount one below each tag. Glue brass disks to sequin pins with industrial-strength craft adhesive to make tacks.

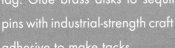

9

Fishing IN CANADA

by Susan Jorgensen

Adhere patterned paper to a piece of mat board. Cut and adhere another patterned paper to cover the top third of the mat board. Conceal the seam with a ruler sticker. Double- and triple-mat your photographs using patterned paper and card stock. Cut out an illustration from patterned paper and insert it in a small metal frame. Apply alphabet and number stickers to round metal frames to create a title. String typewriter keys on some twine. Arrange all the pieces on the background, add a die-cut silhouette, and adhere. Insert in the frame.

OFF *Road*

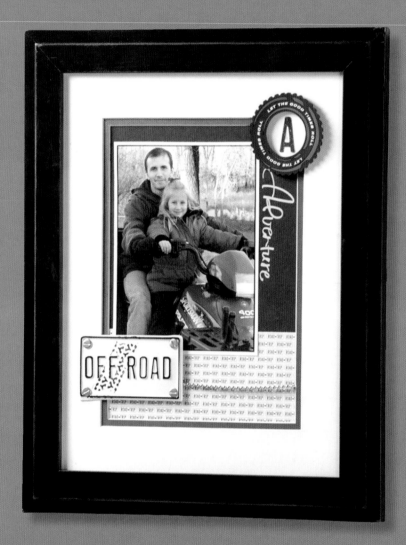

by Nancy Burke

Lightly sand and distress the edges of a painted wooden frame. Apply a matte finish spray. Cover the bottom third of a piece of mat board with patterned paper, add a double-layered mat, and insert in the frame. Adhere a photo in the upper-left corner. Punch a hole at each lower side edge. Thread a metal chain through the holes and tape the ends on the back. Affix a letter sticker to card stock, mount a rubber tire sticker over it, and adhere to the collage. Add a rub-on word along one edge of the photo. Add screw eyes and a tire tread sticker to a small license plate; accent the tire treads with black acrylic paint. Attach the license plate with foam mounting tape.

PEBBLE *Beach*

by Dawn Anderson

Print text for a small photo onto patterned paper. Adhere the photo above the text and trim the paper to create a border. Adhere the bordered photo to card stock and trim ⅛" from the edges. Apply rub-on lettering to a precut mat to create a title. Attach a large photo and the bordered small photo to the mat; use an adhesive foam square where the photos overlap. Attach a golf bag tag at one side. Insert in the frame.

Ocean Isle
BEACH

by Gina Hamann

Arrange and adhere five or six assorted patterned papers to cover a piece of foam core. Cut out words for the title from another patterned paper and chalk the edges. (On a computer, choose the mirror-image printing option and print the title onto the plain side of the patterned paper.) Adhere the title words, a piece of fishing net, shells, small photos, and a sticker verse to the background. Attach a large main photo over the net. Insert in the frame. This layout also works well on a large canvas.

BEACH HOUSE *Summer*

by Gina Hamann

Cover about two-thirds of a piece of foam core with striped paper and the remainder with coordinating solid paper. Conceal the join with scrapbook molding accented with metal eyelets. Lay out photos on the surface to plan your arrangement. Use the solid paper to create single, double, or triple mats for the larger photos, sanding and chalking each mat before adhering the layers. Create a collage in the remaining spaces with a starfish plaque and message, a handwritten verse accented with charms, and a die-cut sand castle (chalked for a muted effect). Insert in the frame. String seashells on two lengths of hemp cord and glue them to the frame.

I LOVE EVERY PART OF *You*

by Gina Hamann

Paint a canvas with acrylic or latex paint and let dry. Wipe white paint around the canvas edges with a paper towel. Cut two patterned papers to overlap one another and fill the center of the canvas, allowing a 1¼" margin all around. Tear the overlapping edge, chalk all the edges, and adhere the papers to the canvas. Mount your large main photo on card stock and trim to create a narrow border. Cut close-ups from additional photos. Punch squares from solid paper and stamp letters on them to spell out a message. Arrange all the pieces on the background and adhere in place, using raised glue dots to make the letters stand out.

When they placed you in my arms,
you slipped into my heart.
—Anne Peterson

Grace LYNN

by Gina Hamann

Machine sew pieces of two different patterned papers together, adhere firmly to a piece of foam core, and trim off excess. Mount a piece of patterned paper onto card stock and sew around the edges. Knot letter charms on ribbon to spell the baby's name. Adhere the name, several ribbon-tied flower buttons, and metal corners to the stitched card. Print a quote onto solid paper; trim and mount on card stock. Print baby photos on canvas cloth, mount on card stock, and tie one with ribbon. Knead two packages of oven-bake clay until soft and warm. Shape one lump into an oval and make an imprint of the baby's foot. Shape the other into a circle and make an imprint of baby's hand. Bake both pieces and let cool, following the manufacturer's instructions. Attach the quote strip at an angle with brads. Add the photos, clay imprints (use ample glue), and name card. Use fibers to tie on a metal label holder with the baby's birth date, weight, and length. The collage will be heavy; be sure to mount it firmly in the shadow box.

Ashley

by Nancy Burke

Spray paint an unfinished wood frame. Ink the edges of a piece of mat board with an ink dauber. Adhere various patterned papers to the mat board, shading the edges with ink. Print the main photo onto canvas, apply preservative spray, and let dry. Mat the photo with card stock, inking the edges of both pieces for a sepia-tone effect, and mount on the background. Print the name using foam stamps and craft paint. Adhere patterned paper to a wooden initial, ink the edges, and attach lace trim. Add the initial and some delicate paper flowers to the collage. Adhere a smaller photo at a slight angle. Run lace trim diagonally across one corner and secure the ends on the back. Insert in the frame.

Sisters

by Gina Hamann

Paint a canvas and let dry. Shade the outer edges with chalk ink. Cut and mount a piece of solid paper in the center. Layer three different patterned papers on this background to form a display area for the photo and then adhere the photo. Fold over the edge of one of the papers and secure with decorative brads. Add eyelets above and below the photo and run ribbon through them, taping the ends on the back. Punch five 1¼" squares and five 1" squares from patterned paper. Sand and lightly chalk the edges. Mount a small square on each larger square, insert a flower brad in the center, and adhere to one edge of the display area. Stamp a title across the top with paint. String beads onto wire, staple the ends to the canvas, and hang from a decorative drawer pull.

Garden SHUTTER

by Nicole Johnson,
Creative Designer, Archiver's

Glue wood accents to the tops of a pair of shutters. Paint the accents and shutters, let dry overnight, and sand the edges to distress the finish. Crop flower photos to the desired size. Print several vintage seed packet images. Cut them out and chalk the edges. Cut a tag from card stock to fit inside a rice paper pocket, and tie on lace trim and ribbon. Arrange the photos and seed packets in the louvers. Add a dragonfly charm and artificial hydrangea.

Precious

BABY

by Nicole Johnson, Creative Designer, Archiver's

For the frame with only one photo, cut patterned paper to fit a piece of mat board. Chalk the edges of small paper flowers and adhere them to the patterned paper. Lay tulle over the entire page. Machine stitch a diamond quilting pattern. Trim off the extra tulle and adhere the paper to the mat board. Cut one set of double mats and a small strip from card stock. Color the edges with chalk ink. Write a date on the strip. Double-mat the photo, turning the top mat slightly askew. Mount the matted photo onto the background at an angle. Attach the date strip and flowers. Insert in the frame and secure a ribbon hanger to the back. Hang from a flower drawer pull.

For the frame with multiple photos, cut patterned paper to fit a piece of mat board. Gather a width of tulle at the middle and tie loosely with thread. Lay the tulle on the paper at a diagonal, machine stitch it to the edges, and trim excess. Mount the paper onto the mat board. Cut two sets of double mats from card stock—one set for a large photo and one set for smaller photos. Color the edges of the mats and small paper flowers with chalk ink. Double-mat a larger photo, turning the top mat slightly askew. Attach paper flowers at one corner. Double-mat smaller photos as a group. Adhere the photos over the tulle. Paint a small oval frame, attach it to the tulle over the thread, and add flowers. Paint metal lettering, rub with chalk ink, and attach. Insert in the frame. Secure a ribbon hanger to the back, and hang from a flower drawer pull.

so sweet

It's a girl...a little beauty,
an angel, and I'm
madly in love with her

Ballerina CANVAS

by Christine Falk

Cut a piece of card stock to fit your canvas. Stamp a harlequin pattern on one area of the card stock and stamp script writing in the remaining area. Affix a grosgrain ribbon and bow to separate the two sections. Paint chipboard letters to spell your ballerina's name and adhere them sideways over the harlequin pattern. Mount a photo onto the script background. Frame the photo with strips of card stock, mitering the corners. Add jewels all around and accent with a chipboard word or phrase. Mount a sticker quote on card stock. Attach it beneath the photo, place a metal ID plate over it, and secure with flower brads. Attach an organdy ribbon and ribbon slides across the top of the collage. Mount the finished page onto canvas using tacky tape.

Graduation
AUTOGRAPH MAT

by Saralyn Ewald, Sr. Designer, Archiver's

Cut white art paper to fit a large frame. Adhere patterned paper to the left third of the art paper, tearing the edge that overlaps. Run ribbon and fiber along the torn edge and tape the ends tightly to the back. Frame two small photos and adhere them to the ribbon with double-sided tape. Slide circle clips around additional small photos and adhere them to the fiber. Double-mat a graduation photo on card stock and patterned paper, using foam adhesive between the two mats for dimension. Mount the photo on the art paper. Use rub-on numbers to add the graduation year. Let friends and family sign the page, and then slide it into the frame for display.

Friends
MAGNETIC MEMO BOARD

by Saralyn Ewald, Sr. Designer, Archiver's

Clean an aluminum sheet with rubbing alcohol or mineral spirits to remove any residue. Sand a 1" border around the edges with coarse-grit sandpaper and wipe off the dust. Punch a hole at each top corner using a hammer and a metal hole punch. Paint the sanded edges with a foam brush, making broad, uneven strokes, and let dry. Apply clear acrylic coating over the painted area to prevent scratches. Thread a ribbon through the holes at the top. To make each daisy magnet, punch two holes in an artificial daisy. Paint a metal washer. Thread a ribbon through the daisy holes and pull the ends through to the front. Slip a washer onto both ribbon ends. Tie the ends together in a knot to secure the washer. Attach a round magnet to the back with craft adhesive. Apply sticker letters to vellum, trim to size, and attach small pieces of self-adhesive magnet to the back. Arrange the flowers, some brightly colored magnets, photos, and vellum pieces on the memo board.

Wedding
FAMILY TREE

by Saralyn Ewald, Sr. Designer, Archiver's

Secure a wedding photo in a mat to fit your chosen frame. Using precision-tip scissors, cut several flowers and leaves from patterned paper. Use a computer to print out a large initial. Cut out the letter, apply repositionable adhesive to the right side, and affix it to the plain side of the patterned paper. Cut around and then peel off the paper template. Brush a thin, even coat of binding glue on the back of the cutouts and attach them to the mat. Glue a flower cutout and a piece of ribbon to the letter. Insert wedding photos of the wedding couple's parents into small frames and tie a ribbon to each one. Secure the framed photos and ribbons to the mat with double-sided tape. Slide the embellished mat into the frame.

Beach WEDDING

by Genevieve A. Sterbenz

Use spray adhesive to affix patterned paper to mat board, for the frame inset. Adhere textured paper to a precut mat. Cut an X inside the mat opening from corner to corner in both directions. Fold the triangular flaps onto the back of the mat, trim off the excess, and glue down. Glue four lengths of narrow velvet ribbon around the mat opening, snipping the ends at an angle to miter the corners. Adhere shell beads, pearls, flower-shaped beads, and seed beads to create baroque-style ornamentation along the top and bottom edges of the mat. Mount photos within die-cut frames and adhere them to the inset. Glue a smaller die-cut frame to card stock and apply sticker letters to spell the names of the bride and groom. Write details on the small frames with a marking pen. Insert in the frame.

Georgia, 1911

by Susan Jorgensen

Adhere patterned paper to a piece of mat board. Tear and adhere a second patterned paper to cover the bottom third of the mat board. Double-mat a vintage photo with card stock. Use a computer to print the name and date of your subject on vellum. Tear around the letters of the name, and adhere next to the photo. Mount the date in a small frame tag. Pull a ribbon through a ribbon slide and attach it diagonally at one corner. Attach a small heart charm tied with ribbon at the top of the photograph. Mat and frame the completed page.

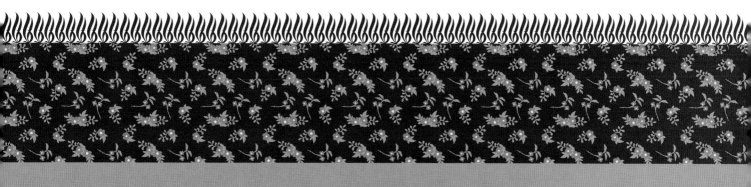

EST *1999*

by Nicole Johnson, Creative Designer, Archiver's

Glue wood accents to the left and right sides of a piece of particleboard. Paint and antique the board and wood letters and numbers that will create your message. Tear a strip of fabric and glue it around the board's outer edges. Cut a piece of foam core to fit between the wood accents. Use spray adhesive to cover the foam core with *matelassé* fabric and layer vintage textiles on top. Adhere a family photo to another piece of foam core, trim to size, and glue ribbon around the edges. Mount the family photo and the wood letters and numbers onto the fabric background. Nail key escutcheons to the board and drill a hole through each one into the particleboard. Knot a ribbon through each escutcheon. Mat small photos on card stock and distress the edges with chalk ink. Wrap small pieces of foam core with fabric, attach the small photos, and hang from the ribbons.

Jakeyboy

by Nicole Johnson,
Creative Designer, Archiver's

Loosely weave strips of twill tape across the front of a piece of mat board and adhere. Mount a large main photo on card stock. Trim the top and bottom edges and tear the side edges of the card stock, leaving an extension on the left. Fold the extension to overlap the photo and tie with a torn fabric strip. Add beads and charms with wire. Mount the matted photo on patterned paper. Cut a strip of the same patterned paper, fold it in half lengthwise, and tear the long edge. Color the torn edge with chalk ink. Wrap the strip around the double-matted photo. Paint metal photo corners and a metal frame and use them to accent several smaller photos. Cut a piece of card stock, texture it with paint and crackle medium, and write a title on it. Stamp the date using chalk ink. Insert in the frame.

MY *Sisters*

by Nicole Johnson,
Creative Designer, Archiver's

Cut a piece of card stock to fit your frame. Crumple the card stock, smooth it out, and rub the surface with an ink pad. Attach eyelets at the corners. Adhere toile fabric on top, pulling loose threads to fray the edges. Cut another piece of card stock, texture it with paint and crackle medium, and chalk the edges. Mat your photo on it and apply sticker letters for the title. Make a black-and-white photocopy of a vintage fabric print. Tear out a selected image, color it with colored pencils, and mount on patterned paper. Layer and fold several pieces of card stock and patterned paper around it to make a decorative paper piece. Rub the edges with chalk ink and glue on coordinating buttons. Insert in the frame.

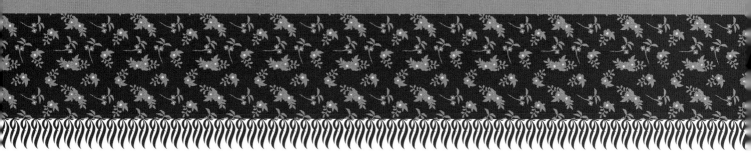

35

Cowgirl

by Dawn Anderson

Adhere patterned paper to a piece of mat board. Mat a large photo on card stock and add leather photo corners. Double-mat a smaller photo on card stock and leather-look paper and add brads at the corners. Mount both photos onto the background. Add a Time Tag Sticker to a page tab. Cut a ⅜" slit in the mat board along the upper edge of the large photo and insert the page tab. Paint a jigsaw alphabet letter and hang it from the tab using a short piece of chain. Use a computer to print the title onto card stock. Cut the title to size, ink the edges, and attach it to a label holder. Install decorative brads in the label holder, tie twine around the brads, and secure the ends to the back of the mat board. Insert in the frame.

THE *Lake*

by Nicole Johnson,
Creative Designer, Archiver's

Enlarge a scenic photo, mount it onto foam core with spray adhesive, and place it in a rustic-looking frame. Cut mats for smaller accent photos from card stock. Distress the mats with chalk ink, mount the photos, and attach them to one edge of the frame. Wrap leather strapping around the frame and accent photos and secure the ends on the back. Paint several skeleton leaves. Cut a piece of card stock to fit a small oval nameplate. Stamp the date on the card stock and distress it with chalk ink. Attach the nameplate and leaves to the frame.

L•O•V•E Frames

by Saralyn Ewald, Sr. Designer, Archiver's

Disassemble four frames. Apply a thick, even coat of bookbinding glue to the front of one frame. Lay the frame, glue side down, on the plain side of a patterned paper with multiple textures, and press to adhere. Turn the frame over and smooth out any air bubbles. Repeat for each frame and let dry. Trim the excess paper even with the frame edges. Sand the cut edges and wipe off the dust. Coat each frame liberally with water-based sealer and let dry. Rub chalk ink around four patterned card-stock letters. Apply double-sided tape to the back of each letter and press onto the decorative side of patterned paper. Cut out each letter with precision-tip scissors, allowing a thin paper border to remain. Attach the letters to the photos with double-sided tape and insert each photo in its frame.

Baseball
GAME

by Christine Falk

Sand, stain, and seal a wooden frame. Punch a series of holes in card stock and sew from hole to hole with red floss to simulate a baseball's stitching. Adhere white paper to the mat board, mount the stitched card stock on top, and secure in the frame. Double-mat your photos using assorted patterned papers. Cut and mat backgrounds for the year and title and attach the number and letter stickers. Ink the edges of each piece with a sponge. Make a tag from card stock, inscribe it, and tie it around the main photo with hemp twine. Arrange and mount all the pieces on the background, using foam dots for the center photo to raise it off the surface. Add leather photo corners, a small leather frame, and a baseball cleat sticker. Tap nails into the top outside edge of the frame and tie on a rawhide lace. Hang the frame from a baseball drawer pull.

Benny
AND CHUMLY

by Susan Jorgensen

Adhere patterned paper to a piece of mat board. Layer and adhere patterned vellum over the top two-thirds and another patterned paper over the bottom third. Conceal the seam with a strip of patterned paper. Mat two small photos on card stock. Cut tea-stained linen fabric ½" larger than each card-stock piece. Mount the matted photos onto the fabric, pull out five or six threads on each side to fringe the edge, and add a brad to each corner. Double-mat a larger main photo with card stock. Slip alphabet tags onto leather laces and wrap them around the main photo. Adhere alphabet stickers to a label, distress the edges with ink, and attach it to the top of the piece. Accent with appropriately themed chipboard words. Insert in the frame.

Slugger

by Nancy Burke

Cut or tear assorted patterned papers for the background, including a piece with a title. Ink the edges, layer on a piece of mat board, and adhere. Cut and attach a piece of a leather baseball. Double-mat the featured photo on card stock, adding photo corners and a ribbon and slide as you work. Using a sewing machine, add a zigzag stitch around the first mat through both layers. Ink the edges, and attach a baseball button to the ribbon slide. Sand a small metal license plate, apply ink, and seal with matte finish. Zigzag stitch thin strips of card stock and ink the edges. Loop the strips through the license plate holes and tape on the back. Mount the license plate with foam tape. Finish the page with appropriately themed tags, stickers, and medals. Insert in the frame.

all BOY

fun at the

park

FUN AT THE *Park*

by Dawn Anderson

Paint a scalloped frame and let dry. Print your desired text onto patterned paper and adhere the paper to a piece of mat board, positioning the text appropriately. Add another piece of patterned paper as necessary to cover the entire surface of the mat board. Double-mat each photo using patterned paper and card stock. Adhere the photos to the background. Add ribbon to conceal the seam in the background papers. Apply cute, chunky clay letters and a chipboard word or two to complete the layout. Install an eyelet word with the date in the lower-right corner. Insert in the frame.

Gearty PARK

by Susan Jorgensen

Sliding in the Park

Adhere patterned paper to a piece of mat board. Mat the photograph on vellum. Paint four decorative brads to match your color scheme and install one at each corner of the photo. String alphabet charms onto ribbon to spell out a title. Drape the ribbon across the top of the collage and tape the ends to the back. Tie a few short strands of ribbon where the title begins. Insert in the frame.

Swinging in the Park

Adhere patterned paper to a piece of mat board. Mat the photograph on vellum. Cut a strip of patterned paper, texture it with a paper crimper, and cut into label strips. Poke a hole at each end and thread with knotted ribbon. Paint small round frames to match your color scheme. Adhere one alphabet sticker to each frame to spell out a title. Attach the frames to the label strips. Run the strips across the bottom of the page and tape the ribbon ends to the back. Insert in the frame.

Pumpkin PATCH

by Susan Jorgensen

Adhere patterned paper to a piece of mat board. Adhere a contrasting paper to the right edge, covering about one-fifth of the surface area. Tear another paper about one-third the size of the surface area and attach it a few inches from the left edge. Cut a phrase from patterned paper for the title and adhere it along the bottom edge. Insert a photo in a small metal frame and adhere it to the center of the collage. Arrange other photographs around it and accent with fabric, brads, label holders, and paper labels. Insert in the frame.

by Dawn Anderson ## *Baby* KEEPSAKES

Baby Footprint Collage

Cover a piece of mat board with two patterned papers and overlay with vellum. Make an ink imprint of the baby's footprint on card stock, trim to size, and ink the edges. Cut patterned paper ¾" larger than the card stock all around. Ink the edges, mount the footprint on it, and adhere to the collage somewhat off-center. Attach a letter sticker of the baby's initial to a small frame holding a mini photo, and adhere the frame to the collage at an angle. Compose a title by stringing letter wraps on ribbon. Insert in the frame.

Keepsake Shadow Box

Create a collage background on mat board with patterned papers and vellum. Adhere a baby photo to patterned paper and trim ¼" from the edges. Paint the frame of a jigsaw alphabet letter and distress with inks. Affix paper to the back of the letter to show through the cutout opening. String letter wraps onto a coordinating ribbon to spell the baby's name. Arrange the photo, letter, ribbon, an oval frame containing a bubble phrase, and the baby's keepsake garments on the collage. Adhere in place inside the shadow box.

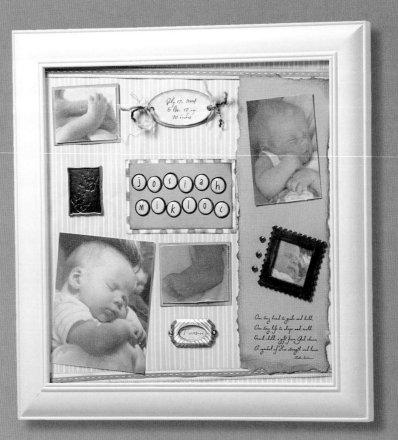

Josiah MIKLOC

by Gina Hamann

Line mat board with patterned paper. Adhere a narrow ribbon to a wider ribbon, and run them at an angle across the top and bottom of the page. Print a verse onto solid paper, trim the paper to cover one-third of the background, and tear and chalk the edges. Print photos onto canvas, cut and adhere paper mats for some, and mount them on the collage. Frame the smallest photo and add brads for accents. Print the baby's birth date and weight on a tag, install eyelets at the sides, and tie with fibers. Add a self-adhesive plaque and label holder. Glue letters to a card to spell the baby's name, and mount on a contrasting mat. Insert in the frame.

Cousins,
ONE A YEAR

by Gina Hamann

Create a collage background on mat board with solid and patterned papers. Cut a patterned strip, sand the edges, and adhere it to conceal the seam. Cut solid paper into pieces slightly larger than several wallet-sized photos. Sand the edges and mat the photos. Label each photo with rub-on letters. Print a title on card stock and insert it in a metal label holder. Run fibers behind the label holder and tape the ends on the back. Mount a transparency of the word *family* on vellum and attach it with brads. Insert in the frame.

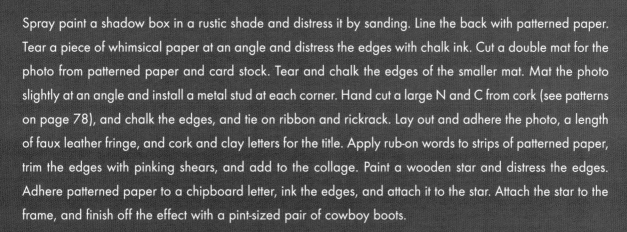

NAKED *Cowboy*

by Nicole Johnson, Creative Designer, Archiver's

Spray paint a shadow box in a rustic shade and distress it by sanding. Line the back with patterned paper. Tear a piece of whimsical paper at an angle and distress the edges with chalk ink. Cut a double mat for the photo from patterned paper and card stock. Tear and chalk the edges of the smaller mat. Mat the photo slightly at an angle and install a metal stud at each corner. Hand cut a large N and C from cork (see patterns on page 78), and chalk the edges, and tie on ribbon and rickrack. Lay out and adhere the photo, a length of faux leather fringe, and cork and clay letters for the title. Apply rub-on words to strips of patterned paper, trim the edges with pinking shears, and add to the collage. Paint a wooden star and distress the edges. Adhere patterned paper to a chipboard letter, ink the edges, and attach it to the star. Attach the star to the frame, and finish off the effect with a pint-sized pair of cowboy boots.

KEY TO MY *Heart* CLIPBOARD

by Saralyn Ewald,
Sr. Designer, Archiver's

Slide a properly sized piece of glass under the clip of a clipboard and make two marks just below the bottom edge of the glass for bolts. Remove the glass and drill a hole at each mark. Apply craft acrylic paint to the clipboard surface with a foam brush using broad, casual strokes. Glue patterned papers to the surface with bookbinding glue. Attach your main photo with double-sided tape and a smaller, framed photo with glue. Compose a message on strips of card stock using a black marker and rub-on transfer letters. Adhere to the clipboard with double-sided tape. Slide the glass into position. Install hex bolts and nuts, but do not overtighten. String a key and a charm onto a metal bead chain and attach the chain to the metal clip. Tie ribbons onto the clip and keyhole.

NEVER LOSE
YOUR SENSE OF *Wonder*

by Gina Hamann

Paint a rectangular canvas and adhere contrasting solid paper to the surface. Enlarge your photo to cover about two-thirds of the background. Mount the photo on solid paper, trim to create a narrow border, and chalk around the edges. Type the words for the title, choose the mirror-image printing option, and print onto white paper. Adhere the white paper to the reverse side of solid paper. Cut out the words and adhere them, right side up, to the collage. Install decorative brads at random. Paint wood letters and let dry. Apply stain and then rub it off for an antiqued look. Attach the letters to the canvas with screw eyes and tie a ribbon at the top of each letter.

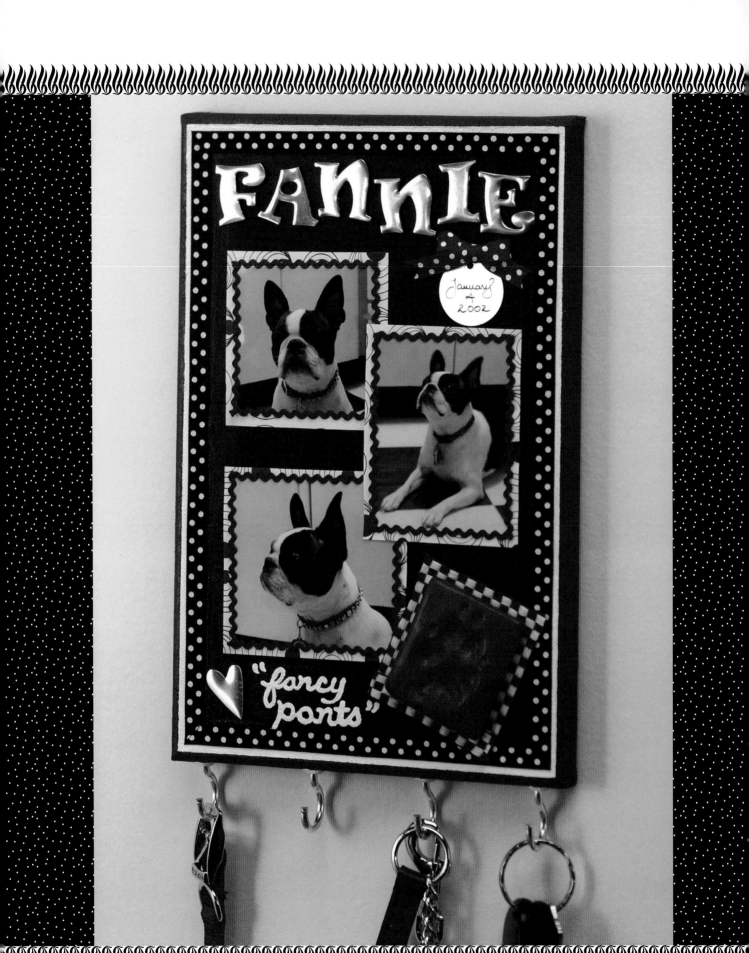

Dog Photo COLLAGE

by Genevieve A. Sterbenz

Apply masking tape to a primed canvas 1/8" from the edge all around. Paint the outer edges and the interior two different colors. Remove the tape when paint is dry. Adhere strips of grosgrain ribbon 1/4" from each edge, mitering the corners. Mat photos on patterned paper and edge with rickrack. Roll out modeling compound to 1/4" thick and make an imprint of your pooch's paw. Cut away excess clay, let dry, and paint. Arrange and adhere photos, the paw print, self-adhesive letters and heart, and a circle charm to the canvas. Frame the paw print with strips of checkerboard trim. Write the dog's nickname with a marker or paint. Screw cup hooks into the bottom edge to hold leashes.

PLAY *Play* PLAY

by Dawn Anderson

Cut a piece of card stock ⅛" larger than each photo all around. Apply ink to the edges of the card stock and center and adhere the photos. Color the center thread of a length of ribbon with a brightly colored marker. Apply rub-ons and a sticker name to tags and rub with acrylic paint. Tie the tags to the ribbon with bead cord and adhere the ribbon to the largest photo. Remove the glass pane from a document frame. Adhere photos to the front of the glass pane. Cut a word strip from a transparency and adhere to the glass at each edge. Reinsert the pane in the frame.

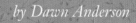

Noah & Madeline

PHOTO TRANSFERS
ON TILES

by Christine Falk

Copy or print photos onto decal paper, trim to size, and apply to ceramic tiles, following the manufacturer's instructions. Let dry several hours. Apply a very light coat of clear acrylic gloss spray sealer and let dry. Repeat the spray sealing process at least two more times. Use spray adhesive to firmly attach dark velvet fabric to mat board and mount in your frame. Add a title to the frame using rub-on letters. Make tags from card stock and chipboard words. Add an eyelet and jump ring to each tag, thread the tags on ribbon, and tie around one tile. Affix the tiles to the velvet background with Goop adhesive. Glue metallic letters to select photos to spell names. Secure each tag with a glue dot.

SPRING *Chicks*

by Dawn Anderson

Tear patterned paper and adhere it to a precut mat. Adhere pieces of foam core to the back for dimension and darken the inside edges of the mat with a marker. Adhere a different patterned paper to mat board for the background. Mount the precut mat onto the background. Double-mat the main photo with card stock and patterned paper and distress the outer border with ink. Mount the photo on a piece of mat board and trim off the excess. Darken the outer edges and attach hinges and a brad. Print a title on patterned paper, cut a tag shape, add a patterned paper border, and install an eyelet. Tie the tag to a hinge with ribbon. Center the main photo in the window opening. Paint the edges of a small frame and rub off the excess. Insert a photo and adhere the small frame to the mat.

Paris
METAL MESH MEMO BOARD

by Saralyn Ewald, Sr. Designer, Archiver's

Disassemble an oval frame. Trace the frame backing onto wire mesh. Cut the mesh with wire snips, set inside the frame to check the size, and clip as needed for a proper fit. Coat the mesh with spray paint, allowing proper drying time on each side. Line the frame rabbet with tacky double-sided tape. Position the mesh inside the frame and press to adhere. Sand and paint a wood fleur-de-lis to match the frame and glue into position. Spell out names of landmarks around the frame using rub-on transfer letters on the frame's flat portion. Use craft adhesive to adhere magnets to the back of round enamel letters. Let dry, and then arrange the letters on the mesh. Tie on photos, postcards, and memorabilia with small pieces of ribbon.

PHOTO TRANSFER
Paris Landmarks

by Genevieve A. Sterbenz

Distress canvases with tea stain and let dry completely. Scan and resize photographs of favorite landmarks to fit each canvas. Print each image onto photo-transfer paper. Cut out the images with deckle-edged scissors and trim off unimportant areas, as if sections of the photo have cracked off or been worn away by time. Fuse each transfer image onto a canvas following the manufacturer's instructions. Write journal notes in the open areas with permanent marker. Use coin mounts and twine to attach coins, or glue coins directly to the canvas.

2 Months

by Nicole Johnson, Creative Designer, Archiver's

Remove the inner panel from a discarded wood-cabinet door. Paint the frame and let dry, and then distress the edges by sanding. Brush on a mixture of equal parts acrylic paint and stain and wipe off with cheesecloth. Paint and antique a wood hanger in the same way and apply a bunny image. Cut foam core to fit the frame opening. Cover the foam core with two patterned papers, tearing the edge that overlaps. Adhere two different patterned papers to a jigsaw number (use a different paper for each piece) and distress the edges with chalk ink. Punch holes at one corner and tie on ribbons and trims. Mat the photo on card stock and chalk the edges. Mount the photo, jigsaw number, and a fanciful array of buttons onto the background and insert in the frame. Attach glass knobs along the lower edge.

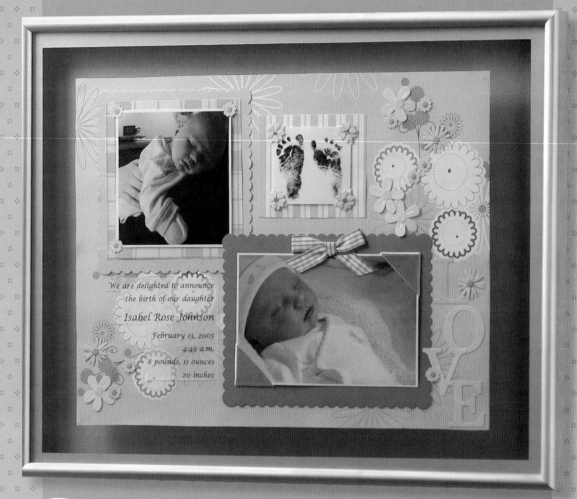

We are delighted to announce
the birth of our daughter
Isabel Rose Johnson
February 13, 2005
4:49 a.m.
8 pounds, 11 ounces
20 inches

Birth ANNOUNCEMENT

by Genevieve A. Sterbenz

Cut patterned paper 1" smaller all around than the glass pane of a document frame. Use photo tape to mount baby and footprint photos onto patterned paper, scallop-edged card stock, or a combination of both. Accent with decorative photo corners or small flowers. Print a birth announcement onto vellum and trim to size. Arrange the collage pieces on the patterned background and embellish with flowers, a ribbon bow, and alphabet stickers. Use double-sided tape to float the collage in the frame.

Baby

by Nicole Johnson,
Creative Designer, Archiver's

Adhere patterned paper to a piece of mat board. Center a smaller piece of a second patterned paper on top. Mat your photo on card stock and trim with a paper edger. Paint a jigsaw letter frame and let dry. Dry-brush the letter frame with white paint and stamp a few flowers. Glue paper to the jigsaw letter, trim off the excess, and distress the edges with chalk ink. Reinsert the jigsaw letter into its frame. Punch a hole at one corner and tie on a tag stamped with the baby's name. Mount the photo and jigsaw letter onto the background. Stamp the remaining letters with foam stamps and acrylic paint. Write the baby's birth date under the title. Embellish with flower buttons. Insert in the frame.

Holiday WREATH

by Nicole Johnson, Creative Designer, Archiver's

Resize photos as needed and insert in 10 assorted small frames. Arrange beaded flowers evenly around the wreath and attach with ribbon or wire. Attach the frames to the wreath to fill in bare spaces. Attach ribbon to the top of the wreath for hanging. Make and attach a double bow with flowing tails.

Memories
PHOTO COLLAGE

by Nicole Johnson,
Creative Designer, Archiver's

Paint over a gilded wood letter and let dry. Sand the edges to let glimpses of the undercoat show through. Adhere patterned paper to a piece of foam core. Arrange photos and the letter on top. Set the letter aside, adhere the photos, and mount the foam core in your frame. Make a tag from card stock and add the family name with rub-on letters. Tie the tag, a tiny oval picture frame, and a silver spoon to the letter with ribbon. Attach extra photos and a metal plaque to the letter. Tack the letter to the background with a needle and fishing line.

Calendar

by Nicole Johnson,
Creative Designer, Archiver's

Adhere chenille fabric to foam core and mount in a frame. Use a computer to create a calendar and a "to do" list. Print onto card stock and cut out. Adhere a strip of patterned paper to the bottom edge of each piece, tearing and chalking the overlapping edge. Layer and adhere two patterned papers for the photo background, concealing the seam with ribbon and a metal rose embellishment. Cut a mat for the photo from card stock, dry-brush the edges with paint, and mount onto the background. Spell out the family name on one side with rub-on letters. Print the word *FAMILY* using foam stamps and paint. Attach all three pieces to the background with decorative pushpins.

Heirloom SCREEN

by Nicole Johnson, Creative Designer, Archiver's

Sand three rectangular pine boards, apply spray paint, and let dry. Cut a piece of wallpaper for each panel. Hinge the panels together. Apply the wallpaper using spray adhesive. Lay the screen flat and arrange a variety of heirloom items on the panels. Mount hardware for picture frames, drawer pulls, plate hangers, and escutcheons by nailing or screwing directly into the wood (drill a starter hole for screws). Attach textiles or lightweight pieces with double-sided tape. Hang framed photos from ribbon. Drill slender holes and thread fishing line through them to tack on heavier items, such as a hand mirror.

≋ MATERIALS LISTS ≋

Our Family
by Gina Hamann

Pg. 7

Canvas: Canvas Concepts

Craft paper

Solid paper, fibers: Bazzill Basics

Solid paper: Canson

Word charms: Karen Foster Design

Eyelets

Screw eyes and hooks

Chalk ink: ColorBox by Clearsnap

Acrylic paint: Crafters Edition

Font: Verdigris, Autumn Leaves

Oval cutter: Creative Memories

Eyelet setting tool and hammer

French Vineyard Shadow Box
by Genevieve A. Sterbenz

Pg. 8

Shadow box

Card stock with scalloped edge

Patterned paper

Suede paper

Postcard

Wine label

Champagne glass and wine bottle stickers, die-cut grapes and leaves: Jolee's By You, EK Success

Wine cork

Small stone

Raised glue dots: Pop-Up Glue Dots, Glue Dots Adhesive Products

Travel Shadow Box
by Saralyn Ewald

Pg. 9

Shadow box: Structural Industries

Corrugated cardboard

Card stock, vellum: Anchor Paper

Patterned paper, letter stickers: Karen Foster Design

Patterned paper: Penny Black

Printed map

Yosemite National Park sticker

Chipboard letter: The Art Department with Sara Tumpane, Li'l Davis Designs

Brass disks: EK Success

Sequin pins: Dritz

Antique letter stamps

Black ink: StazOn, Tsukineko

Chalk ink: ColorBox "Chestnut Roan" by Clearsnap

Fine-tip black marker

Foam adhesive dots: All Night Media, Plaid

Industrial-strength craft adhesive: E6000

Fishing in Canada
by Susan Jorgensen

Pg. 11

Frame

Mat board to fit frame

Card stock

Patterned paper: Karen Foster Design; Sticker Studio

Small metal frame: Making Memories

Round metal frames

Typewriter keys

Alphabet, number, and ruler stickers: Sticko, EK Success

Die-cut boat silhouette

Twine

Off Road
by Nancy Burke

Pg. 12

Frame

Precut or custom-cut double mat

Mat board to fit frame

Card stock

Patterned paper, letter stickers, rubber tire sticker, tire tread sticker, metal license plate: Road Trip Collection and Scrap Pl8, both from Sticker Studio

Metal bead chain

Screw eyes

Rub-on word: Déjà Views

Black acrylic paint: Delta Technical Coating

Matte finish spray: Krylon

Foam mounting tape: 3M

Hammer and metal hole punch

Pebble Beach
by Dawn Anderson

Pg. 13

Frame

Precut mat to fit frame

Card stock

Patterned paper: Heidi Grace Designs

Rub-on letters: Making Memories

Golf bag tag

Font: Updated Classic, Autumn Leaves

Adhesive foam square: PeelnStick by Therm O Web

Ocean Isle Beach
by Gina Hamann

Pg. 15

Frame

Foam core to fit frame

Patterned paper: BasicGrey

Fishing net, shells: US Shell Inc.

Sticker: Cloud 9 Design

Chalk ink: ColorBox "Chestnut Roan" by Clearsnap

Font: Gettysburg, Autumn Leaves

Beach House Summer
by Gina Hamann

Pg. 16

Frame

Foam core to fit frame

Striped paper, solid paper, scrapbook molding: Chatterbox

Solid paper: Die Cuts with a View

Starfish plaque, metal eyelets, metal charm letters: Making Memories

Die-cut castle: Jolee's By You, EK Success

Hemp cord: Darice

Seashells with natural holes

Chalk ink: ColorBox by Clearsnap

Eyelet setting tool and hammer

I Love Every Part of You
by Gina Hamann

Pg. 17

Canvas: Canvas Concepts
Card Stock
Patterned paper: Chatterbox
Solid paper: Bazzill Basics;
Chatterbox
Stamps: PSX Designs for
Creativity
Chalk ink: ColorBox by
Clearsnap
Acrylic paint: Crafters Edition
Raised glue dots: EK Success
3D Dots
Square punch, ¾": Creative
Memories

Grace Lynn
by Gina Hamann

Pg. 19

Shadow box
Foam core to fit shadow box
(fit snugly because collage is
heavy)
Card stock
Patterned paper: BasicGrey
Solid paper: Chatterbox
Canvas cloth: Office Depot
Oven-bake polymer clay:
Sculpey
Brads, flower buttons, metal
corners, metal label holder:
Making Memories
Letter charms
Ribbon: EK Success
Fiber
Fonts: Crumbly Gingersnap
by Melissa Baxter; Verdigris,
Autumn Leaves
Glue: Magic Scraps Scrappy
Glue

Ashley
by Nancy Burke

Pg. 20

Unfinished wood frame
Mat board to fit frame
Card stock
Patterned paper: Diane's
Daughters
Canvas: Fredrix Artists' Canvas
by Tara Materials, Inc.
Wooden initial: Wal-Mart
Paper flowers: Robin's Nest
Crocheted lace trim: Fibers by
the Yard
Foam alphabet stamps:
Making Memories
Ink pad: Archival Ink "Sepia,"
Ranger Industries
Latex spray paint: Krylon
Preservative spray: Preserve
It! Digital Photo and Paper
Protectant, Krylon
Acrylic craft paint
Ink dauber

Sisters
by Gina Hamann

Pg. 21

Canvas: Canvas Concepts
Patterned paper, vellum:
Chatterbox
Solid paper: Bazzill Basics;
Chatterbox
Brads: Bazzill; Making
Memories
Eyelets
Ribbon: EK Success
Assorted beads
24-gauge spool wire
Decorative drawer pull:
Restoration Hardware
Chalk ink: ColorBox by
Clearsnap
Latex paint: Benjamin Moore
Square punch, 1" and 1¼":
Creative Memories
Alphabet rubber stamps

Garden Shutter
by Nicole Johnson

Pg. 22

Wood shutters
Wood accents: Walnut Hollow
Card stock
Flower photographs
Seed packets: Seeds to
Sow CD-ROM, the Vintage
Workshop
Rice paper pocket:
Nostalgiques by Rebecca
Sower, EK Success
Dragonfly charm
Ribbon
Lace trim
Artificial hydrangea
Chalk ink: ColorBox "Chestnut
Roan" by Clearsnap
Latex paint: Benjamin Moore

Precious Baby
by Nicole Johnson

Pg. 23

Frame
Mat board to fit frame
Patterned paper: 7gypsies
Card stock
Tulle: Jo-Ann
Thread
Paper flowers: Jolee's By You,
EK Success
Small metal oval frame
Metal alphabet and "Baby"
word: Making Memories
Ribbon
Flower drawer pull
Acrylic paint: Delta Ceramcoat
Chalk ink: ColorBox "Chestnut
Roan" by Clearsnap

Ballerina Canvas
by Christine Falk

Pg. 25

Canvas: Canvas Concepts
Card stock
Chipboard letters, jewels:
Heidi Swapp by Advantus
Corporation
Chipboard words: the Art
Department with Sara
Tumpane, Li'l Davis Designs
"Girls" quote sticker: Autumn
Leaves
Metal ID plate: Art Warehouse
by Creative Imaginations
Heart ribbon slides: Maya
Road
Mini flower brads: Making
Memories
Grosgrain ribbon
Organdy ribbon
Rubber stamps: Hero Arts
Rubber Stamps Inc.
Pigment ink stamp pad
Acrylic paint

**Graduation
Autograph Mat**
by Saralyn Ewald

Pg. 26

Frame
Art paper: Canson
Card stock
Patterned paper: Phresh &
Phunky Collection, Basic Grey
Fibers: On the Surface Fibers
"Indigo," Croppin' Paradise
Scrapbooks
Circle clips, small frames,
ribbon, rub-ons: Making
Memories
Marker: Zebra Rollerball
Foam adhesive

Friends Magnetic Memo Board
by Saralyn Ewald

Pg. 27

Aluminum sheet

Clear vellum: Anchor Paper

Faux gerbera daisies: Michaels

Letter stickers: Monogram Series, American Crafts

Colored magnets

Ribbon: May Arts

Self-adhesive magnetic sheets

½" magnet discs: ProMAG, Dick Blick

Washers: Making Memories Washer Words "friendship"

Acrylic paint: FolkArt, Plaid

Acrylic coating: Krylon "Crystal Clear"

Industrial-strength craft adhesive: E6000

Hammer and metal hole punch

Wedding Family Tree
by Saralyn Ewald

Pg. 29

Frame

Precut or custom-cut mat

Patterned paper: Daisy D's

Round silver frames: I Kan'dee Keepsake Pocket, Pebbles Inc.

Ribbon: Li'l Davis Designs

Precision-tip scissors: EK Success

Beach Wedding
by Genevieve A. Sterbenz

Pg. 30

Frame

Precut or custom-cut mat

Mat board to fit frame

Card stock

Patterned paper, die-cut reversible frames, letter stickers: Anna Griffin

Textured paper

Velvet ribbon

Pearls

Seed beads

Oval shell beads

Flower-shaped beads

Marking pen

Georgia, 1911
by Susan Jorgensen

Pg. 31

Frame

Precut or custom-cut double mat

Mat board to fit frame

Card stock

Patterned paper: 7gypsies; Foofala, Autumn Leaves

Vellum

Ribbon

Frame tag, ribbon slide: Nunn Design

Heart charm

Font: Kunstler Script

EST 1999
by Nicole Johnson

Pg. 33

½"-thick particleboard

Wood accents: Walnut Hollow

Foam core

Card stock

Floral fabrics: Ralph Lauren

Matelassé fabric

Wood letters, wood numbers, ribbons: Michaels

Key escutcheons: Rockler

Vintage doily

Vintage kitchen towel

Chalk ink: ColorBox "Chestnut Roan" by Clearsnap

Acrylic paint: Delta Ceramcoat

Latex paint: Hirschfield's

Antiquing polish: FolkArt, Plaid

Jakeyboy
by Nicole Johnson

Pg. 34

Frame

Mat board to fit frame

Card stock

Patterned paper: 7gypsies

Twill tape

Torn fabric strip

Metal photo corners, metal frame: Making Memories

Metal charm

Beads

Wire

Small alphabet and number stamps: Hero Arts Rubber Stamps Inc.

Chalk ink: ColorBox "Chestnut Roan" by Clearsnap

Pen: Slick Writer, American Crafts

Acrylic paint: Delta Ceramcoat

Crackle medium: FolkArt, Plaid

My Sisters
by Nicole Johnson

Pg. 35

Frame

Card stock

Patterned paper: 7gypsies

Alphabet stickers: Nostalgiques by Rebecca Sower, EK Success

Toile fabric: Jo-Ann

Vintage child's-print fabric

Buttons: SEI

Eyelets, circle clip: Making Memories

Acrylic paint: Delta Ceramcoat

Crackle medium: FolkArt, Plaid

Chalk ink: ColorBox "Chestnut Roan" by Clearsnap

Colored pencils: Staedtler, Dick Blick

Ink: VersaMark, Tsukineko

Eyelet setting tool and hammer

Cowgirl
by Dawn Anderson

Pg. 37

Frame

Mat board to fit frame

Card stock

Leather-look paper

Patterned paper: 7gypsies

Decorative brads, jigsaw alphabet, leather corners, label holder: Making Memories

Brads: Lasting Impressions

Page Tab, Time Tag Sticker: Nunn Design

Small chain

Handmade sisal twine: Provo Craft

Acrylic paint: Americana, DecoArt

Ink pad: Archival Ink, Ranger Industries

Font: ITC Viner Hand, Microsoft

The Lake
by Nicole Johnson

Pg. 38

Rough cedar frame: Michaels

Foam core to fit frame

Card stock

Leather strapping

Skeleton leaves: All Night Media, Plaid

Metal nameplate: Making Memories

Number stamps: Hero Arts Rubber Stamps Inc.

Chalk ink: ColorBox "Chestnut Roan" by Clearsnap

Acrylic paint: Delta Ceramcoat

L•O•V•E Frames
by Saralyn Ewald

Pg. 39

Frames: IKEA

Patterned paper: Phresh & Phunky Collection, Basic Grey

Card stock letters: Vagabond Collection, BasicGrey

Chalk ink: ColorBox "French Blue" by Clearsnap

Water-based matte finish sealer: Mod Podge, Plaid

Bookbinding glue, neutral pH: Lineco, Dick Blick

Precision-tip scissors

Baseball Game
by Christine Falk

Pg. 41

Frame: Walnut Hollow

Mat board to fit frame

Card stock

Patterned paper: Karen Foster Designs; Paper Pizazz

White paper

Red embroidery floss

Leather photo corners, leather frame: Making Memories

Alphabet and number stickers: Road Trip, Sticker Studio

Baseball cleat sticker: Jolee's Boutique Major League Baseball, EK Success

Baseball glove rawhide lace

Hemp twine

Eyelet

Baseball drawer pull

Dark brown ink pad

Walnut wood stain

Clear satin polyurethane

Foam dots

Punch tool

Eyelet setting tool and hammer

Benny and Chumly
by Susan Jorgensen

Pg. 42

Frame

Mat board to fit frame

Card stock

Patterned papers: Nostalgiques by Rebecca Sower, EK Success; Sticker Studio

Patterned vellum

Chipboard words: the Art Department with Sara Tupane, Li'l Davis Designs

Brads: Making Memories

Tea-stained linen fabric

Leather-textured tag stock sticker label: Sticker Studio

Alphabet stickers: Frances Meyer

Leather lacing

Metal alphabet tags

Ink pad: Ranger Industries

Slugger
by Nancy Burke

Pg. 43

Wood frame

Mat board to fit frame

Card stock

Patterned paper: Sticker Studio Baseball

"All American" sticker, Scrap Pl8 metal license plate, sports medal, tag: Sticker Studio

Photo corners: Pioneer

Baseball button: Jesse James & Co., Inc.

Ribbon: Fibers by the Yard

Ribbon slide

Hemp twine

Ink pad: Archival Ink "Sepia," Ranger Industries

Matte finish spray: Krylon

Fun at the Park
by Dawn Anderson

Pg. 45

Scalloped frame

Mat board to fit frame

Card stock

Patterned paper: Bo-Bunny Press; Cloud 9 Design

Eyelet word, ribbon: Making Memories

Chipboard words, clay alphabet: Li'l Davis Designs

Acrylic paint: Americana, DecoArt

Font: Handcrafted, Autumn Leaves

Eyelet setting tool and hammer

Gearty Park
by Susan Jorgensen

Pg. 46

Sliding in the Park

Frame

Mat board to fit frame

Patterned paper

Vellum

Alphabet charms: American Traditional

Ribbon: Adornments by K1C2, LLC, EK Success

Decorative brads: Making Memories

Acrylic paint: FolkArt, Plaid

Pg. 46

Swinging in the Park

Frame

Mat board to fit frame

Patterned paper: Marah Johnson, Creative Imaginations

Vellum

Round metal frames

Round alphabet stickers: K&Company

Ribbon: Making Memories

Acrylic paint: FolkArt, Plaid

Paper crimper: Fiskars, Dick Blick

Pumpkin Patch
by Susan Jorgensen

Pg. 47

Frame

Mat board to fit frame

Patterned papers: Bo-Bunny Press; Cloud 9 Design; Scrapworks

Brads, charmed frame, label holder: Making Memories

Fabric label: Me & My Big Ideas

Baby Keepsakes
by Dawn Anderson

Pg. 49

Baby Footprint Collage

Frame

Mat board to fit frame

Card stock

Patterned paper: BasicGrey; Foofala, Autumn Leaves; Me & My Big Ideas

Vellum: Mrs. Grossman's

Ribbon: May Arts

Ribbon Charm Letter Wraps: Making Memories

Small metal frame: Marcella by Kay

Alphabet letter sticker for frame: K&Company

Ink: Marvy Matchables, Uchida of America Corp.; Ancient Page, Clearsnap

Pg. 49

Keepsake Shadow Box

Shadow box

Mat board to fit frame

Patterned paper: BasicGrey; Foofala, Autumn Leaves

Patterned vellum: Walter Knabe, Paper Adventures; The Sharon Ann Collection, Déjà Views

Ribbon: May Arts

Jigsaw alphabet, ribbon Charm Letter Wraps: Making Memories

Bubble phrases, oval metal frames: Li'l Davis Designs

Baby keepsake garments

Acrylic paint: Americana, DecoArt

Ink: Marvy Matchables, Uchida of America Corp.; Ancient Page, Clearsnap

Josiah Mikloc
by Gina Hamann

Pg. 50

Frame

Mat board to fit frame

Canvas cloth for printing photos: Office Depot

Patterned paper, tag: Chatterbox

Solid paper: Bazzill Basics

Metal frame, metal letters: Jo-Ann

Brads, Charmed plaque, eyelets, ribbon: Making Memories

Label holder: Nostalgiques by Rebecca Sower, EK Success

Ribbon: Textured Trios, Michaels

Fibers: BasicGrey

Chalk ink: ColorBox by Clearsnap

Fonts: Sandra, Autumn Leaves; Renaissance, Creating Keepsakes

Eyelet setting tool and hammer

Cousins, One a Year
by Gina Hamann

Pg. 51

Frame

Mat board to fit frame

Card stock

Patterned paper: SEI

Solid paper: Chatterbox

Vellum: Paper Pizazz

Brads, metal label holder, rub-ons: Making Memories

Transparency: Sweetwater

Fibers: Bazzill Basics

Fonts: Artsy by Melissa Baxter; Sandra, Autumn Leaves

Naked Cowboy
by Nicole Johnson

Pg. 53

Shadow box: Structural Industries

Card stock

Patterned paper: Anna Griffin; EK Success; Flair Designs

Cork: Boone (Use the N and C patterns on page 78.)

Clay alphabets, rub-ons: Li'l Davis

Jigsaw chipboard alphabets: Making Memories

Cowboy boots

Wood star: Provo Craft

Metal studs

Ribbon: Textured Trios, Michaels

Rickrack: Wrights

Faux leather fringe

Chalk ink: ColorBox "Chestnut Roan" by Clearsnap

Acrylic paint: Delta Ceramcoat

Spray paint: Krylon

Key to My Heart Clipboard
by Saralyn Ewald

Pg. 54

Clipboard: Saunders

Glass

Hex bolts with nuts

Card stock

Patterned paper: Life's Journey, K&Company; Rusty Pickle

Acrylic paint, bead chain, leather frame, rub-ons: Making Memories

Charm: I Kan'dee, Pebbles Inc.

Ribbon: Life's Journeys, K&Company; Li'l Davis Designs

Key

Fine-tip black marker

Bookbinding glue, neutral pH: Lineco, Dick Blick

Electric drill with ¼" drill bit

Never Lose Your Sense of Wonder
by Gina Hamann

Pg. 55

Canvas: Canvas Concepts

Solid paper: Bazzill Basics; Canson

Wood letters: Michaels

Ribbon

Screw eyes

Snowflake brads

Chalk ink: ColorBox by Clearsnap

Gel wood stain: Home Décor by Delta

Acrylic paint: Crafters Edition

Dog Photo Collage
by Genevieve A. Sterbenz

Pg. 57

Canvas: Canvas Concepts

Patterned paper

Modeling compound: Model Magic by Crayola

Self-adhesive letters, heart: Petals and Possibilities Scrap Metal

Circle charm: Making Memories

Ribbon

Rickrack

Checkerboard trim

Brass cup hooks

Acrylic paint

Play Play Play
by Dawn Anderson

Pg. 58

Document frame

Card stock

Color transparency: Danelle Johnson for Art Warehouse, Creative Imaginations

Large flat tag: Nunn Design

Small colored metal tag

Ribbon: Making Memories

Bead cord: Anna Griffin

Numeric rub-ons: Scrapperware Karen Burniston, Creative Imaginations

Name sticker: It Takes Two

Yellow marker: Zig, EK Success

Ink: Memories, Stewart Superior Corp.

Acrylic paint: Americana, DecoArt

Noah and Madeline Photo Transfers on Tiles
by Christine Falk

Pg. 59

Black frame with 15" x 15" opening

15" x 15" mat board

White card stock

½ yard of black velvet fabric

4 white ceramic tiles, 6" x 6"

Decal paper: Waterslide Decal Paper for Inkjet Printers by Lazertran

Ribbon, rub-on letters: Making Memories

Lowercase metallic alphabet: Metallix, KI Memories

Chipboard words: the Art Department with Sara Tumpane, Li'l Davis Designs

7mm jump rings: Jewelry Designer by Darice

Eyelets

Spray sealer: Patricia Nimocks Clear Acrylic Sealer, Plaid

Adhesive: Goop

Computer, scanner, and inkjet printer

Eyelet setting tool and hammer

Spring Chicks
by Dawn Anderson

Pg. 61

Frame

Precut or custom-cut mat

Mat board to fit frame plus extra

Foam core

Card stock

Patterned paper: Bo-Bunny Press; Enchanted Complements by the Crafter's Workshop; 7gypsies

Charmed frame, eyelet, hinges, ribbon: Making Memories

Brad: Lasting Impressions

Acrylic paint: Americana, DecoArt

Ink: Ancient Page, Clearsnap

Marker: Zig, EK Success

Font: Lucida Calligraphy, Microsoft

Perfect Paper Adhesive, Matte: US Art Quest

Eyelet setting tool and hammer

Paris Metal Mesh Memo Board
by Saralyn Ewald

Pg. 62

Oval frame

Wood fleur-de-lis: Artistic Appliqués

Galvanized hardware cloth, ½" mesh, 19-gauge

Patterned paper (Paris map): Me & My Big Ideas

Enamel alphabets: Leeza Gibbons Legacies

½" magnet discs: ProMAG, Dick Blick

Ribbon, rub-ons: Making Memories

Eiffel Tower sticker: Traveler's Stickers, Pier 1 Imports

Spray paint: American Accents "Heirloom White," Rust-Oleum

Acrylic paint for fleur-de-lis: Winsor & Newton

Industrial-strength craft adhesive: E6000

Wire snips

Photo Transfer Paris Landmarks
by Genevieve A. Sterbenz

Pg. 63

Canvas: Canvas Concepts

Transfer paper: Invent It! Ready to Print Iron-On Transfers

Coins

Coin mounts: Nunn Design

Twine

Pekoe black tea (such as Lipton)

Scanner and computer printer

Deckle-edged scissors

---

2 Months
by Nicole Johnson

Pg. 65

Wood-paneled cabinet door: thrift store purchase

Wood hanger: Teeny Step, IQA, Inc., Target

Foam core

Card stock

Patterned paper: Daisy D's; K&Company; 7gypsies

Jigsaw number: Making Memories

Glass knobs: Jo-Ann

Clear mirror buttons: EK success

Plastic and metal buttons

Ribbon and trim

Bunny image: Holiday Collection 1 CD-ROM, the Vintage Workshop

Chalk ink: ColorBox "Chestnut Roan" by Clearsnap

Latex paint: Benjamin Moore

Acrylic paint: Delta Ceramcoat

Staining antiquing medium: DecoArt

Cheesecloth

Birth Announcement
by Genevieve A. Sterbenz

Pg. 66

Silver document frame: Umbra Scribe

Patterned paper: Lime Floral, Snow & Graham

Patterned paper, ribbon photo corners: Laura Ashley, EK Success

Vellum

Scallop-edged card stock

Die-cut alphabet: Tim Coffey, K&Company

Flowers, daisies, glitter green photo corners: Jolee's By You, EK Success

Ribbon

Font: Monotype Corsiva

Baby
by Nicole Johnson

Pg. 67

Frame

Mat board to fit frame

Patterned paper: Bo-Bunny Press; Inspirables by EK Success

Card stock

Flower buttons, jigsaw alphabet, foam stamps: Making Memories

Paper edger

Flower stamp

Tag: Office Max

Ribbon

Alphabet stamps: Hero Arts Rubber Stamps Inc.

Pen: Slick Writer, American Crafts

Chalk ink: ColorBox "Chestnut Roan" by Clearsnap

Acrylic paint: Delta Ceramcoat

Holiday Wreath
by Nicole Johnson

Pg. 69

Wreath
Rectangular frames: Marcella by Kay; Leeza Gibbons Legacies
Oval frames: Carr
Beaded flowers: Jo-Ann
Ribbon for hanging and bow

Memories Photo Collage
by Nicole Johnson

Pg. 70

Frame: Home Images, Michaels
Foam core to fit frame
Card stock
Patterned paper: Anna Griffin
Gilded wood letter
Rub-ons: Making Memories
Small silver oval frame: Blue Moon Beads
Silver spoon
"Family" plaque: Li'l Davis
Ribbon: Li'l Davis, Michaels
Fishing line
Acrylic paint: FolkArt, Plaid

Calendar
by Nicole Johnson

Pg. 70

Antique frame
Foam core to fit frame
Chenille fabric
Card stock
Patterned paper: Daisy D's
Foam stamps, pushpins, rub-ons: Making Memories
Metal rose: Millie and Maude
Ribbon: Textured Trios, Michaels
Acrylic paint: Delta Ceramcoat
Font: Academia, Creating Keepsakes

Heirloom Screen
by Nicole Johnson

Pg. 71

Three 1" x 10" x 24" pine boards
Wallpaper: Brunschwig & Fils
Vintage and heirloom items (embroidered towel, doily, saucer, spoon, hand mirror)
Drawer pull
Frames: Carr; Marcella by Kay
Hardware, hinges, key escutcheon: Rockler
Key: Westrim
Plate hanger: OOK
Ribbon
Fishing line
Spray paint: Krylon
Double-sided tape: 3M

Patterns for Naked Cowboy, page 53

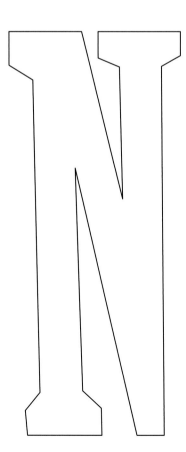

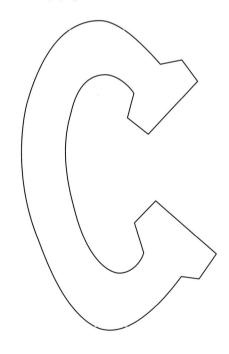

RESOURCES

Visit these Web sites to view and learn more about scrapbooking products, including many featured in this book.

American Crafts
www.americancrafts.com

American Traditional
www.americantraditional.com

Anchor Paper
www.anchorpaper.com

Anna Griffin
www.annagriffin.com
Store locator by zip code.

Autumn Leaves
www.autumnleaves.com
No ordering on this Web site.

BasicGrey
www.basicgrey.com
Store locator by zip code or shop online stores.

Bazzill Basics
www.bazzillbasics.com
Web site is wholesale only, but browsers are welcome.

Blue Moon Beads
www.bluemoonbeads.com
Web site is wholesale only; call 1-800-377-6715 to find a retailer near you.

Bo-Bunny Press
www.bobunny.com
Store locator on Web site.

Canson
www.canson-us.com
Store locator by zip code.

Canvas Concepts
www.canvasconcepts.com
Store locator on Web site.

Chatterbox
www.chatterboxinc.com
Store locator by zip code.

Clearsnap
www.clearsnap.com

Cloud 9 Design
www.cloud9design.biz

Crafter's Workshop, The
www.thecraftersworkshop.com

Crayola
www.crayolastore.com

Creative Imaginations
www.cigift.com

Creative Memories
www.creativememories.com

Croppin' Paradise Scrapbooks
www.croppinparadise.com

Daisy D's
www.daisydspaper.com

DecoArt
www.decoart.com
Stores, online vendors, and mail-order vendors listed on Web site.

Déjà Views
www.dejaviews.com

Delta
www.deltacrafts.com
Store locator by zip code.

Diane's Daughters
www.dianesdaughters.com

Dick Blick
www.dickblick.com

Die Cuts with a View
www.diecutswithaview.com
Store locator on Web site.

EK Success
www.eksuccess.com
Store locator by zip code.

Fibers by the Yard
www.fbty.com

Frances Meyer
www.francesmeyer.com
Store locator on Web site.

Glue Dots Adhesive Products
www.gluedot.com

Heidi Grace Designs
www.heidigrace.com
Store locator on Web site.

Heidi Swapp by Advantus Corporation
www.heidiswapp.com

Hero Arts Rubber Stamps
www.heroarts.com

IKEA
www.ikea.com

It Takes Two
www.ittakestwo.com
Stores and online vendors listed on Web site.

Jo-Ann
www.joann.com

K&Company
www.kandcompany.com
Store locator by zip code.

KI Memories
www.kimemories.com
Stores and online vendors listed on Web site.

Krylon
www.krylon.com

Lasting Impressions
www.lastingimpressions.com
Store locator by zip code.

Lazertran
www.lazertran.com

Leeza Gibbons Legacies
www.leezagibbonslegacies.com
Store locator by zip code.

Loew-Cornell
www.loew-cornell.com

Making Memories
www.makingmemories.com

Maya Road
www.mayaroad.com

Me & My Big Ideas
www.meandmybigideas.com
Store locator by zip code.

Memories
www.memories.com
Shop online or at a Memories retail store.

Michaels
www.michaels.com

Mrs. Grossman's
www.mrsgrossmans.com

Nunn Design
www.nunndesign.com
Contact info; to see images, visit www.kiwiscraps.com.

OOK
www.ooks.com
Wholesale only on Web site.

Paper Adventures
www.paperadventures.com
Store locator or shop online.

Pebbles Inc.
www.pebblesinc.com
Store locator on Web site.

Pioneer
www.pioneerphotoalbums.com
No ordering or store finder on this Web site.

Plaid
www.plaidonline.com

Provo Craft
www.provocraft.com
Store locator by zip code.

Ranger Industries
www.rangerink.com
Store locator or shop online.

Rockler
www.rockler.com

Rust-Oleum
www.rustoleum.com
Store locator or shop online.

Rusty Pickle
www.rustypickle.com
Store locator or shop online.

Saunders
www.saunders-usa.com

Scrapbook.com Superstore
www.scrapbook.com
Shop online.

Scrapbooking Top 50
www.scrapbookingtop50.com
Links to the top 50 scrapbooking sites for online shopping. Rankings updated daily.

Scrapworks
www.scrapworks.com
Store locator on Web site.

Sculpey
www.sculpey.com

7gypsies
www.sevengypsies.com
Site is wholesale only, but visit to see the products.

Stewart Superior Corp.
www.stewartsuperior.com
Link to an online vendor.

Sticker Studio
www.stickerstudio.com
Link to an online vendor.

Structural Industries
www.structuralindustries.com
List of major chain retailers.

Tara Materials, Inc.
www.taramaterials.com

Therm O Web
www.thermoweb.com

3M
www.3m.com

Tsukineko
www.tsukineko.com
Store locator by zip code.

Two Peas in a Bucket
www.twopeasinabucket.com

Uchida of America Corp.
www.uchida.com
Store locator by zip code.

US Art Quest
www.usartquest.com

Vintage Workshop, The
www.thevintageworkshop.com

Walnut Hollow
www.walnuthollow.com

Westrim Crafts
www.westrimcrafts.com

Winsor & Newton
www.winsornewton.com
Store locator on Web site.

Wrights
www.wrights.com
Stores and online vendors listed on Web site.

Zebra
www.zebrapen.com
Links to online vendors.

ABOUT THE DESIGNERS

Dawn Anderson
Dawn Anderson has worked in the publishing industry for 12 years and especially enjoys the opportunity to develop craft books as an editor at Martingale & Company. Her designs have been published in a variety of books and magazines over the years, including *Collage Cards: 45 Great Greetings!* and *Party Time! Making Invitations, Favors, and Decorations*, published by Martingale & Company. Dawn enjoys decorating with photos and often uses family photos in place of artwork throughout her home.

Nancy Burke
Nancy Burke has been a professional scrapbook and lettering designer for eight years, and she enjoys all forms of arts and crafts. Her work has been featured in many books and magazines, and she is a designer for several product design teams. She has taught all over the country and is a designer member of the Craft and Hobby Organization and the Society of Creative Designers. As the owner of Scrap 'N' Ink Co., a recently launched design firm, she hopes to continue to share her love of scrapbooking with students as well as manufacturers in the scrapbooking and hobby industry. Nancy lives in Meridian, Idaho, with her husband, daughters, and numerous beloved pets.

Saralyn Ewald
Saralyn Ewald has a BFA in ceramics and loves to create art and explore different mediums. She gets to indulge in her current passion, paper crafting, as the senior designer at Archiver's. Saralyn's designs have appeared in several project books, including *Collage Cards: 45 Great Greetings!*, *Layer by Layer: Collage Projects for Home Decorating*, and *Party Time! Making Invitations, Favors, and Decorations*, published by Martingale & Company. She resides in Saint Paul, Minnesota.

Christine Falk
Christine Falk has always had an interest in crafts and interior decorating, and she enjoys creating projects for publication. Her recent project designs can be found in *Layer by Layer: Collage Projects for Home Decorating* and *Party Time! Making Invitations, Favors, and Decorations* published by Martingale & Company. During her 12-year career as a freelance editor, she produced newsletters and worked on self-published poetry books. Christine resides in Lakeville, Minnesota, with her husband and two teenage children. Much of her spare time is spent with her family, golfing, traveling, biking, hiking, and dabbling in her newest hobby—photography.

Gina Hamann
Gina Hamann's seven-year passion for scrapbooking is inspired by a much greater passion: her family. Gina writes: "I am so blessed with an incredible husband and three beautiful children. I love to create meaningful pages that express my feelings for them and then watch them get excited about the pages." Gina's work as a scrapbook consultant has given her the opportunity to help others capture their memories and tell the stories of their lives. Her hobbies include training for rollerblade marathons, biking, gardening, and "any outdoor activity."

Nicole Johnson
Nicole Johnson learned how to sew doll clothes when she was eight years old, and she has been designing and enjoying crafts ever since. She started scrapbooking when her oldest daughter was born. A few years later, in 2002, Nicole left a career in the interior design field and joined Archiver's, first as a lead instructor and more recently as a creative designer in the corporate office. Nicole especially loves "junktiques," crafts made by creating something new from something old. She is convinced that her passion for creativity has affected her children, observing that her daughters will often see some random item and say, "Mom, can't you use that for *something*?"

Susan Jorgensen
Susan Jorgensen has been involved in the visual design field for many years, mainly in the photography and film industry. Her love of photography made scrapbooking a natural choice, and she has also worked on many books featuring crafts and sewing. In her spare time, Susan enjoys gardening, sewing, reading, biking, swimming, hiking, and spending time with her 11-year-old daughter.

Genevieve A. Sterbenz
Genevieve A. Sterbenz is the author of seven craft and home-decorating books. She is a contributing designer to books, magazines, and newspapers, and is a frequent guest on television programs, where she presents decorating ideas. Some of her designs can be found in *Layer by Layer: Collage Projects for Home Decorating* and *Party Time! Making Invitations, Favors, and Decorations* published by Martingale & Company. As the founder of Greenbean Productions, Genevieve creates custom scrapbooks, keepsake photo albums, invitations, and giftwrap designs for private clients. She lives in New York City.

CONTRIBUTORS

A special thanks to the contributors whose products were used in this book.

Advantus Corporation (Heidi Swapp)
Autumn Leaves (Foofala)
Bo-Bunny Press
Canvas Concepts
DecoArt

EK Success
Hero Arts Rubber Stamps
Lazertran
Loew-Cornell
Maya Road

Nunn Design
/gypsies
Sticker Studio
Therm O Web
Walnut Hollow